Hybrid C…

Blen…

and Offli… …nity

CW01623898

Peter Phillips

Director, Centre for Digital Theology, Durham University

Head of Digital Theology for Premier Christian Media

GROVE BOOKS LIMITED

RIDLEY HALL RD CAMBRIDGE CB3 9HU

Contents

For all those engaged in the ministry of the church during COVID-19—lay and ordained—who have learnt new skills, worked through the night and gone beyond your own comfort zones to bring church outside the walls of our closed buildings. Techies, liturgists, evangelists and pastors, may God bless you abundantly for all you have done and all you continue to do.

Church Mission Society supports the Grove Mission and Evangelism Series
At Church Mission Society, we believe that every Christian is called to join in God's mission, whether that means crossing the street or crossing continents, and we want to set people free to put that call into action.

The cover image is copyright © Grove Books Ltd

Copyright © Peter Phillips 2020

First Impression August 2020
ISSN 2399-6536
ISBN 978 1 78827 126 4

Introduction from Peter Phillips

1

A Church Without Walls

March 2020 saw the enforced closure of churches, an event almost unprecedented in British history. Only once before, in 1209, have all the churches been closed, because of the interdict of Pope Innocent III who instructed priests to go on strike over King John's refusal to accept Stephen Langton as the Archbishop of Canterbury. That closure lasted for six years—but baptisms and the last rites were permitted.

Church buildings closed at the end of March 2020 but, emphatically, the church has not closed. The church continues to worship, pastor, minister, pray and love both online and offline, across any kind of technology it can use, both analogue and digital. The Centre for Digital Theology at Durham University has been well placed to see this as a global phenomenon.[1] We have been engaged in conversations around the world during the pandemic and the same seems to be true everywhere. The church has taken every opportunity it can to switch to a distributed model. We have been unable to use our buildings, but we have made use of every channel possible to preach the good news about Jesus, to provide for the needs of the community, to worship God.

Since last September I have been working closely as a digital/missional consultant with *Sanctuary First*, an online church network with a passion for creative resources that is part of Falkirk Presbytery of the Church of Scotland.[2] *Sanctuary First* is headed up by Albert Bogle, former Moderator of the Church of Scotland and strong advocate of their 2001 report 'A Church without Walls.'[3] That report focused on the missiological need of the church to move beyond institutionalism and buildings and out into the beyond where Jesus was found to be on mission. One of the closing paragraphs puts it well:

> A Reformation that put Jesus Christ above every religious convention, deconstructed the ecclesiastical pecking order and turned a static-gathered church into a mobile-scattered church, who began to find Jesus beyond our walls in strangely 'unholy' places—now that would be a Reformation worthy of the name.

This booklet ties in well with the report and the work of pioneers like *Sanctuary First*. We need to get out of our buildings and find God in the wild.

In Many Instalments and in Many Ways

Mission is a multichannel activity—perhaps because God is so keen to express his love for the world in so many different ways. It is, in the end and at the beginning, his mission. And of course, God uses all methods and all channels for mission. In Eph 1.23 we hear that God fills all things in every way—or rather 'all in all' (English needs the 'things' to make sense but it spoils the imprecision of the Greek). This passage is indeed about the church, his body; but the reference to the filling of all things (the *pleroma*) is about God's own identity and activity. This is picked up again later in the letter, in Eph 4.23, where we hear that the God and Father of all is over all, through all and in all. God's use of creation itself as a witness to his own nature has been made clear in Paul's Letter to the Romans (chapter 1), and the pre-eminence of the Son as a witness to the fullness of God is described in Colossians (1.19; 2.9). The plurality of channels which God uses for mission, and the particularity of the role of Christ for that mission, is set out in the wonderful opening of the Letter to Hebrews (1.1–3a):

> In the past God spoke to our ancestors through the prophets at many times and in various ways, but in these last days he has spoken to us by his Son, whom he appointed heir of all things, and through whom also he made the universe. The Son is the radiance of God's glory and the exact representation of his being, sustaining all things by his powerful word.

The two Greek words opening this passage which describe God's missional activity fit well with what has happened during the COVID-19 pandemic—*polumerōs kai polutropōs*—'in many times and in many ways,' or perhaps, 'in many bits and in many ways' since the first word means that God's mission has come to us in many instalments. Unlike Paul on the Damascus Road who seemed to encounter everything at once, God provides us with lots of pictures of his work, through the work of the prophets and patriarchs, through faithful women down the ages, through old and young, through royalty and commoners, through many different races. During the pandemic the church has witnessed to God's mission 'in many instalments and in many ways.' Through my research I have seen how diverse the church's mission has been during the virus, and this is what we hope to explore in subsequent chapters.

From live-streamed services from their buildings in the early days of lockdown in March, the church quickly diversified into Facebook Live and YouTube-streamed live celebrations, video compilation services or pre-recorded services, and gallery-view Zoom celebrations, during which households can gather around a screen to see other church members whilst various hosts lead different parts of the service. Using Zoom you can even send people off into breakout rooms for discussions or prayer. There are youth groups using Minecraft for their Bible studies and *Alpha* has jumped online across the world. Others have provided phone and/or text-based services, with clergy mastering Twilio to arrange telephone links to YouTube or Zoom audio streams, or recording sermons as MP3s. Some have hand-delivered orders of service around their village. Some have celebrated kitchen-table eucharists—a fascinating reincarnation of such celebrations by both non-conformists and Roman Catholics during the late Reformation. Roman Catholic priests have streamed masses by the million, or gathered people on Zoom to say offices, or the rosary, or sing songs. But at the same time as doing the above, the church has helped in COVID-19 support groups, run foodbanks, managed care for the homeless, met people on the streets, supported single parents, worked as chaplains in hospitals, prayed for the sick, visited the elderly in a socially distanced way, set up pastoral conversations by phone or letter and written to parishioners. Daily services are regularly available from many different sources and the disabled church, who had taken to online ministry ages ago as a place of their own choosing, has come into its own.

The church has continued to witness to the mission of God despite buildings being closed

In many instalments and in many ways, the church has continued to witness to the mission of God to all people despite buildings being closed. We have seen 'A Church without Walls' move from a Church of Scotland report to an almost universal experience of contemporary Christianity—with many saying that they do not want to turn the clock back. This transformation has become obvious as the different chapters of this book popped into my inbox. What each contributor aims to show is how God is leading them in their own missional engagement—either online, offline, hybrid, public, anonymous, using whatever technology necessary or none. So this book is about God's mission continuing during a pandemic, a church beyond walls, rather than just about digital communication, or God online.

God in the Wild

Whilst it is important to reflect on the role of the church at this time, we also need to remember that God's mission is much bigger than us. He has a whole creation to evangelize. And so the polls which show a rise in engagement with online services and an increase in prayer as part of contemporary culture will in part be about online services, but also about the sovereign activity of God in the wild. The numbers of those viewing services is surrounded by complex issues of how you count such views, but various micro-research projects have now shown pretty strongly that the SavantaComRes figures, suggesting up to a threefold increase in interest in church services/activities (from 7% to 25%), are close the truth.[4] People do drop in and out of services (as we all do when attending in person, no doubt) but there is also significant growth in engagement with Bible studies, daily offices and other discipleship opportunities. These are harder to dip in and out of by the nature of how they are run. Moreover, as many of the daily offices are on Facebook Live or Zoom, the presenter can see the names of those attending.

This increase has me asking what God is up to. When I did some research on Google Trends to track keywords around spirituality and God, I found that online services were a small part of the search ecology. Much bigger were the words 'prayer,' 'Jesus' and 'God.' Despite people in relatively secular Britain thinking that God is old-fashioned, currently God seems to be more popular and people are showing increased interest. Is this part of God's own self-revelation in contemporary culture? It is not just the impact of lots of services online. When people have time on their hands, they search for God, they bump into God, and they find God out searching for them. When you are faced with the horrors of a pandemic and social isolation, God might present himself as the best answer to your inner needs.

When people have time on their hands, they search for God

This search for the presence of God is paralleled in my own research into the Bible on social media, where I noted a drift from doctrinal verses to therapeutic verses over a decade of lists of the most popular Bible verses searched for, highlighted and shared on such platforms.[5] Both YouVersion and BibleGateway (the two big players in this field) have also recently noted a shift in Bible searching over the pandemic. Instead of verses focused on an individual's activity to improve their own lives (therapy), suddenly the verses are all God-centric, with God as the subject of the verbs, with God as the initiator of our therapy. Whilst this shift may possibly be a short-term contextual adjustment, it is perhaps another sign of the rise in interest in God's activity during the pandemic or, more theologically, a sign of God in the wild.

God's mission is confined neither to online nor offline church—indeed that distinction is increasingly redundant. Though the mission of the church is part of the mission of God, God's mission is not limited to our mission. In our contemporary world we need to remember that the majority of society is digitally engaged—whether they are poor or rich, young or old. I know from personal experience that there are many in the church who talk of the digital divide, but the figures from OfCom[6] and the ONS paint a slightly different picture—of nearly universal penetration of the digital in terms of device ownership and digital access.[7] Whilst it is true that a third of those over 65 are less likely to use the internet and almost a half of those over 75, the ONS found that less than 10% of all UK adults could be termed non-users back in 2018.[8] With such high proportions of our society online, God is already reaching out to where people are, on digital channels and social media.

To engage effectively in the mission of God over the internet, the church needs to work harder at understanding the materiality of online ministry. Everybody who appears on Zoom or YouTube is an offline, enfleshed human being. None of us are virtual, none of us are digital. We are all ordinary people whose images are turned into data and reassembled on screens. God reaches out to us in many different instalments and in many different ways. The church needs to witness across multiple channels that the world might hear of God's grace and love. Thank God that we are involved in both digital and analogue ministries, both in ministry offered online and enfleshed in the world.

Hybrid Approaches

For this book I have invited three practising ministers to share what they have been doing to enable people to meet with God, and also to reflect upon the mission of God, the self-revelation of God, of God in the wild. Knowing these people would normally explore innovation through digital means, I made the assumption that their stories would be of digital engagement. Instead, each of them shows how they have developed a decidedly hybrid approach focusing more on mission beyond the limitations of a building—a genuine *church without walls*.

2

Reflections from Bryony Taylor

God for All

Online Church is Real Church

When the UK went into lockdown on 23 March 2020, I was in some respects well prepared for moving ministry online. From past experience I already knew the benefits and what might work and what might not. Suddenly people who had previously looked down upon social media as something lesser (particularly for Christians to use) were livestreaming services and enthusiastically embracing technology.

During the lockdown, Christians and church leaders have discovered that online church can be real church. The old designation of IRL (in real life) versus virtual has been shown to be false—life online is just as real as face to face, in-person life. It might be different, but it is not any the less real. Christians (especially in the comfortable West) during the pandemic have been forced to test what they have always been taught, that the church is not the building but the people (1 Cor 3.9), and that there is nowhere that God cannot be present (Ps 139.7–12). The disabled community, in particular, has known this for a long time. This revelation has implications for how we view mission and how God might be at work as the world shifts and changes in response to the pandemic. Here I hope to share and reflect on some observations from my own experience as an Anglican priest in my parishes in two ex-mining communities in North East Derbyshire.

Now We Have a Bigger Net

In 2010 Craig Von Buseck published a book called *Netcasters: Using the Internet to Make Fishers of Men.*[9] I was reminded of this title as I watched people engaging with online worship during lockdown. In particular I noticed a trend of the spouses of some regular attendees of our church services on a Sunday (who I have never met) beginning to engage enthusiastically. One gentleman, being more technically minded than his wife, set about becoming the cameraman so that she could do a reading for inclusion in a pre-recorded service. He has now set up a home system so that they can watch Sunday services on their television and they both attend our Sunday morning coffee meetings on Zoom. Previously I had never seen him in church. Another woman, the wife of another regular, never attended church services in person but has been one of the most prolific commenters and likers of my posts in our church Facebook group.[10] There is something about the fishing net online that can catch more fish than the net we use in our church buildings. Most of us know this to be true because the viewing figures of our online services far exceed the numbers that usually attend in person. I am interested, however, not in the big numbers but in the one or two (like these two examples) who have become more engaged with church than they have ever been; they have been caught up in the net. I am interested to see how we can keep them once we have returned in some form to worship in our buildings.

Deeper Discipleship

The deprivations of lockdown have deepened people's discipleship. At the outset people were encouraged to create a daily routine, and I took the opportunity to inspire my congregations to make time for prayer each day as a way of getting through this tough period. My congregations are typical English middle of the road Anglicans who generally do not talk about their faith or attend many Bible studies—it is not their usual practice. However, since lockdown, both those who have used a printed prayer booklet that I distributed to all who do not have internet access *and* those engaging online have told me how much more praying they have done. They have also watched other online services, television and radio broadcasts, not just those that I have offered.

It is not only the natural turning towards God in times of crisis that is taking place, however. I took the deliberate decision to create forms of worship online that I would not be able to do in our buildings, trying to make the most of the fact we are not restricted by four walls.[11] In aiming to be as inclusive as possible, I also launched a 'dial a sermon' system for those without the internet to enable them to listen to sermons over the telephone. I have had interesting feedback on this. A number of people are listening to the sermon more than once—ringing on a Sunday and then again later in the week. Without the distractions of being able to see other people, and of the microphone perhaps not working properly, some people are able to focus more on the sermon on the telephone. What might first appear to be a lesser form—preaching for audio only—actually offers real benefits for some and is even better than their usual experience in our church building. In addition, online services on YouTube can be watched with captions—those who would usually miss much of what takes place in the church building because they are hard of hearing can now understand everything and are no longer excluded. I have been deeply encouraged by seeing people grow in their faith during this pandemic and hope we can draw lessons from this for the future.

Boldness

> Pray also for me, so that when I speak, a message may be given to me to make known with boldness the mystery of the gospel. (Eph 6.19)

It is easier to be bold and direct online or in print than it is face to face. British people tend not to want to speak openly about religion. We find direct expressions of faith cringeworthy. Anthropologist Kate Fox speaks about this in her book *Watching the English*: 'Earnestness of any kind makes us squirm. Religious earnestness makes us deeply suspicious and decidedly twitchy.'[12] This is as true for Christian ministers as it is for parishioners. Being online, however, provides the opportunity for us to be more open and bold about our faith without fear of immediate embarrassment or ridicule.[13] I discovered this in my research in 2015 into how people share their faith online—people feel less embarrassed asking about faith in an online setting, especially in private messaging, than they would coming to speak to me at the end of a Sunday service.[14]

In online worship, I feel I can be bolder in my preaching and teaching and parishioners feel more confident about sharing such worship on the internet with friends and family. Bringing someone physically to a church service is far more intimidating than sending a link to a YouTube clip saying, 'You might like this.' Many of my offline parishioners have written to friends and shared our dial-a-sermon number with them—people who live in other parts of the country and from other denominations. I have joked with those who listen that if they get bored with my sermon they can hang up and I will never know! Although this is a joke, it is actually the reason why more people are being reached through these different forms of worship—the ability to switch off if you do not like it makes people give it a try in the first place. To continue the fishing metaphor, the option to switch off is actually the bait.

Lessons for the Future

I mentioned previously in this chapter how the disabled community has known for a long time of the value of online church. We must, as a church, learn the lessons of inclusivity from this time of pandemic and not go back to excluding those who cannot attend worship in our buildings. This means we will need to move to a more mixed economy in terms of our worship and mission. I often say that I have both an online congregation and an offline one—and both are equally important. The overlap used to be quite small but it is widening, and now incorporating curious observers, as more people are using technologies such as YouTube, Zoom and Facebook.

We must learn the lessons of inclusivity from this time of pandemic

Why would we not use the bigger, more efficient fishing net provided by the internet to reach increasing numbers of people with the gospel once we are allowed back into our buildings? Why go back to using a less effective fishing method and reach fewer people? The new things I have set up during the pandemic I intend to continue even when we return to our buildings because I have seen people's discipleship deepen, new people engaging with the faith (both from within our church community, like the spouses mentioned above, and further afield) and an increased boldness in sharing faith. In the future, we will need a hybrid model of church to serve the online and offline congregations as well as curious observers. We will continue with dial a sermon, some form of weekly live online service and a service in our church building, and I wonder where we will see the most growth? It might not be in returning to our old fishing grounds, but reaching out into new waters. 'When *Jesus* had finished speaking he said to Simon, "Put out into deep water and let down your nets for a catch"' (Luke 5.4).

3

Reflections from Matthew Pulis

Digitally Mediated Rosary

The Rosary

The rosary is a Catholic devotional practice which clearly has stood the test of time. Simply put, the rosary involves five decades of Hail Marys while meditating on five events from Christ's life. Each decade is encapsulated with an 'Our Father' and 'Gloria' at each end. This devotional practice was already well established by the mid-sixteenth century. Although the rosary is the Marian prayer *par excellence*, it involves reflection and meditation on the life of Christ.[15] In essence, it is a 'participation in the life of Mary, whose focus was Christ,' as Romano Guardini aptly summarizes it.[16]

Marian Tradition in Malta

Marian tradition on the Roman Catholic Island of Malta is ubiquitous. Since St Paul's shipwreck on our shores as reported in Acts 28, Malta has remained predominantly Christian. World War history has also reinforced this Marian tradition. For example every Assumption Day (15 August) we commemorate *Operation Pedestal*, a convoy of ships which in 1942 brought much-needed food and goods to besieged Malta. Many to date still see this event as a miraculous Marian deliverance. Of the 494 Catholic churches on the island, 214 are dedicated to Mary and 11 parishes are dedicated to the Assumption of Mary, one of which is Dingli.

The Dingli Parish

Dingli is considered to be one of the more remote villages in Malta. Although it is a mere five-minute drive from urban Rabat, the cultural shift made in that short journey is pronounced. Dingli is very rural, and many of the elderly still tend their own smallholdings. However, it has also recently seen an increase of young Maltese families buying property,[17] which has brought the average age down to 37.2.[18]

Fr Mark Mallia Pawley, the parish priest, faced two conundrums: an elderly and often lonely generation, and an upcoming generation (40% of the parish) aged under 30. It is in this scenario that COVID-19 has hit the village. The parish's main challenge, therefore, has been how to remain physically close to the elderly in a time of social distancing, who are very limited in their internet usage, while keeping a daily engagement with the younger folk. In this time of disorientation, it made sense to revert to a Marian theme for missionary work, and so emerged the idea of streaming the rosary in the public square.

Streamed Digital Rosaries

The parish was split into 8 zones, each covering a hamlet or so, and every Wednesday and Friday, the parish priest and I, together with a small technical team, would go to each hamlet's central point to recite the rosary there. We broadcast the rosary using loudspeakers, and half an hour in advance, we began inviting people to come out from their windows, doors, roofs or balconies to join us in prayer. Keeping social distance was of the utmost importance, and at times proved difficult, since some elderly people would naturally approach us or their neighbours, so we kept having to remind them of the importance of safeguarding each other. The rosary was then streamed live using audio from our Facebook page, where an average of 50 households would join us online to pray this communal prayer. Our main aim was to maintain the devotional practice of reciting of the rosary, a pious prayer often associated with lay people rather than clergy, as both crucial outreach and pastoral ministry. Moreover, this hybrid digitally-mediated rosary allowed us to pray together with our parish both out on the road and online.

The bi-weekly recital of the rosary was accompanied by a Monday gathering of five families from the parish, who would join an online video conference call (like Zoom), where they would recite the rosary, whilst also being joined by an average of 30 households on Facebook Live. This event was targeted more towards the younger generation, and so most families involved were of altar boys or children already engaged with the parish. We noticed that the elderly, wanting to see their nephews and nieces reciting the rosary, would ask for assistance to set up Facebook on their smartphones, computers or TVs to join us from around Malta.

All the different digitally-mediated rosaries helped the parish to feel more united in a time of social isolation. As explained, some of the older generation asked other family members to help them get online so as to be close to the parish and be able to pray together. In a sense, it is now the younger generation who are teaching the elderly how to approach prayer, reversing the usual roles involved in building the faith community. Moreover, those who were previously beyond the reach of online efforts are being included by the clergy visiting their remote hamlets to broadcast the rosary.

Theological Inspirations

The impetus for the parish to opt for a Marian piety goes beyond traditional reasons to embrace more theological ones. The three main theological inspirations were adopted from Pope Francis' prayer for the pandemic first recited when he visited the Salus Romani shrine: the visit itself; the 'sign of hope'; and Mary's command at Cana, 'Do whatever he tells you.'[19]

The Visit to the Shrine

Shrine pilgrimages have been part of the Catholic tradition since the fourth century. The pilgrimage itself is not primarily the destination but more about the journey towards the destination, where one contemplates one's life and faith. Speaking of pilgrims, Pope Francis notes that they are the 'immune system of the church,' and emphasizes the need for the priest at shrines to be welcoming.[20]

In this time of pandemic, we are observing another reversal of roles. It is us priests who are the pilgrims to the shrines of our hamlets. It is we who are walking towards the sacred space where the rosary will be recited and joined by the villagers from their doorsteps. In this pilgrimage, we are reminding people that their households are sacred spaces, and it is the *domus ecclesiae* which is being highlighted over the baroque-adorned brick and mortar church—incarnational missiology in practice. Our pilgrimage invites those living with family to reflect on their identity as Christians called to pray together at home, and move away from an ill-understood sacramental ecclesiology which sees prayer as an individual effort rather than a communal one. The danger of individuality presents the lay person as a consumer of the sacraments, whereas our Christian faith advocates a theology of the gift of the free meal as explored by Thomas O'Loughlin: 'In liturgy we are not consumers, but celebrants.'[21] Likewise, in the liturgy celebrated in the *domus ecclesiae*, often mediated through the digital, those who partake truly become the celebrant and invite the Holy Spirit to transform their house not merely into a home, but a church.

'Sign of Hope'

In one of the most important documents issued by the Catholic Church during the Second Vatican Council, the Roman Church adorns Mary, the figure and model of the church, as 'a sign of certain hope and comfort to the pilgrim people of God.'[22] In a period of disorientation, reverting back to the sure sign of hope is inevitable for a Catholic. And this is not the first time during a pandemic that Catholics have approached Mary for her mediation. In the Black Plague, Christians developed the second part of the Hail Mary to seek Mary's help and protection from the disease. Fulton Sheen explains that this addition suggests a 'spontaneous outcry of people in a great calamity.'[23] This is explained by the 'now' and 'at the hour of our death' clauses, as both moments were almost synonymous to fourteenth century Christians.

In his prayers for the pandemic, Pope Francis suggests that we pray the intercession of Mary to comfort those who are distraught and 'be close to those who are concerned for their loved ones who are sick and who, in order to prevent the spread of the disease, cannot be close to them.'[24] It is this closeness which inspired us to set up our physical/digital recital of the rosary. Given the hundreds of elderly people, maybe feeling forgotten and disconnected from the digital world, as priests we wanted to become in ourselves a Marian embodiment of the sign of hope. Mary's *spoude* (haste and 'eagerness and diligence') on her journey to accompany Elisabeth became our inspiration to visit the elderly and get as close as we possibly could without endangering their health (Luke 1.39–40).[25] One criticism might be that just by being there and reciting the rosary we were not offering much help to the loneliness-stricken generation, but what assistance could pregnant Mary offer to Elisabeth, save that of hope-filled accompaniment? In a similar manner we wanted our visits to be symbols of the dawning tomorrow.

'Do Whatever He Tells You'

During May, Catholic tradition suggests attending more closely to the school of Mary and contemplating Christ's life through her eyes through the rosary. These words are more relevant than ever during the pandemic. In his gospel, the powerful last words of Mary recorded by John are, 'Do whatever he tells you' (John 2.5), a challenge of Mary to all Christians across the centuries. Also in John, the last words of Christ, 'Follow me,' echo down the years as an invitation to trust in Christ and commit one another into God's merciful hands (John 21.23).

In a parish which is stricken by a high sense of loneliness, the mere echo of the parish priest's voice reciting the rosary is a balm to isolated people's solitude and thus exercises the ministry of consolation. Our presence was not interpreted only as the leader of a community present amongst his people, but somewhat that Christ as the shepherd of his flock was present. In a time where people feel disoriented, Christ's shepherd-like figure becomes even more urgent.

Digital and Physical Rosaries

When we were exploring how we could best address the pastoral needs of our parish, we began by offering specific events depending on the age and needs. On a weekly basis, we held web conferences with the altar boys, streamed interactive homilies for the young ones, communal liturgies of the hours via web conferencing and Sunday masses as well as digital catechesis. However, while half of the parish's population was being addressed through such social media opportunities, the elderly were not. Although the parish priest had telephoned all the older parishioners, in our Mediterranean culture the physical is paramount, and so we were inspired to broadcast the Facebook rosaries physically in each hamlet.

Two final points which helped us discern the way forward are relevant for those of every denomination to reflect on.

- We opted for a specific devotional practice often associated with the laity. As most priests, us included, were busy streaming masses, we were concerned about the risk of faith becoming even more clericalized, where the priests 'say' mass and the laity join in a 'spiritual communion' whilst 'hearing' the mass. Thus we opted to use a tradition rooted in popular piety, easily understood by all, and one which was already a familiar practice in the local Catholic tradition pre-COVID-19.
- The choice of broadcasting digital prayer in a physical way helped combat the heightened effects of loneliness created by COVID-19. Given our priority to safeguard the elderly it was impossible to visit them in their homes, but by bringing this event to their doorsteps they felt remembered by their parish priest as well as by Christ. Moreover, we were also addressing the younger generation through online streaming, so while physically we were surrounded by elderly people, digitally we were joined by younger families. This reinforced the reality that we pray together as one community, though we each have our own needs and hopes.

Reflections from Joanne Cox-Darling

4

Gateway God

I spend a lot of time online. I have all the credentials for being part of this wave of online Christians who are using the opportunities of a global pandemic for positive, kingdom-living, Jesus-loving effect. But my response when the pandemic hit was to buy an A-frame chalkboard, some chalk pens and raid my children's craft supplies.

In my context, a leafy part of Staffordshire, the pandemic raised for me the question of how to resource, serve and equip the whole of my community for the long haul. For some, it remains how to access the basic necessities of the day: food; clothing; tackling the technology poverty which is driving an invisible wedge into the heart of our society. For others, most starkly in my mind, was the question of how to resource people to take their souls seriously. To see all the markers of mental health crises and articles on trauma—even noticing the emotional toll on my own well-being and acuity—as an invitation into some soul care.

> **Mission needed to be more open to people's own spirituality and well-being**

A little like David and his slingshot defeat of Goliath, I was going to fight COVID-19 and the associated societal crises, armed with a sense that mission needed to be more gentle, more wise, more hopeful and more open to people's own spirituality and soulful well-being (1 Samuel 17). For me, there is something vital about offering space for people to be themselves in the face of the pandemic, to recognize fear, to live in hope, and to respond with gentleness and respect (1 Pet 3.15).

I wanted to find a physical, embodied, practical, life and breath, taste and touch approach to responding to the pandemic. A prophetic and visceral way to challenge physical distancing and the apparent retreat of the church to the computer screen. An invitation to a holistic, present and presence existence. A hybrid approach which was soul-full, about soul care, missional, full of ritual, the mysteries of the sacred, boundary-pushing in sacramental practices, imperfect, temporary, experiential. Written in chalk. Placed on a wonky, faded, cracked, plastic, green garden table. My altar.

If, as many have identified, a global pandemic is a form of corporate trauma, how might people be offered something to nurture their souls for the long haul of trauma response, anxiety and survival? What might a flesh and blood expression of our aliveness look like in the face of the precise opposite, a deadly virus transmitted through physical contact?

Garden Path Ministry

It is likely that my Methodist theology and natural inclination to push boundaries led me, literally, up the garden path. Methodists proudly declare that 'The world is my parish'—a statement intended to topple ecclesiastical hierarchy in the eighteenth century, but now a permission-giving, rallying call to all things exotically missional.

When lockdown happened, the world started to walk past my driveway in droves. I live on a village main road connecting the city of Wolverhampton to other parts of South Staffordshire. Thus during lockdown, this road became a well-worn route for walkers, runners, families and everyone on their prescribed daily exercise.

People passed by who needed to know that they were seen: that their psyche mattered; that the quirks of lockdown and associated anxieties were real and important; that their souls needed to be considered as much as where to buy toilet paper, flour or yeast. Thus every Sunday morning we put out a different statement and ritual response for people to read, take away—or indeed completely ignore.

We have handed out:[26]

- Seed potatoes (because good things grow in dark places, and it is good to celebrate the dark times with friends in the light). A practice in getting back to creation and nature. Having spent such a long time on Zoom and online platforms, I keep returning to Shane Claiborne's quotation, 'I want to make sure I write emails with dirt under my fingernails.'[27]
- Palm crosses. Being so steeped in postmodernity, and an early practitioner in emerging church experiments, I surprised myself with how amazed I was that the simple act of offering a palm cross on Palm Sunday could actually be the hook the community needed into this chalkboard ministry.
- Easter eggs. An invitation to feast.
- Wooden plaques with the fruits of the Spirit written on them (take what you need, and hold onto it). A gift of characterfulness, and a nudge towards being able to ask for what we need. During the week that crime statistics were released, which showed that 75% of all local crimes were of domestic disturbances, we offered the

same wooden plaques, but with the phone number of the National Domestic Abuse helpline on it. These too were taken.

- Rainbow thank-you decorations. A reminder of living with gratitude.
- Blank postcards to write to loved ones. A reminder that being connected is not always through a video call.
- Origami peace cranes (for VE day, patriotically coloured red, white and blue). An invitation to storytelling and living a peaceable kingdom.
- Wrapped teabags (make a brew and think about who you are becoming). An invitation to live lightly, and to let go a little more.
- Love hearts. This happened in the week of the *#blacklivesmatter* movement coming to the fore, so we connected with injustice and anger, and the willingness to do better and to be better.
- Stones to paint and add to the large stone labyrinth temporarily taking up the church car park nearby, because we are all pilgrims on a journey, finding beauty in the cracks. An invitation to holding memory and remembrance.
- Well-being retreat packs—bags filled with coloured papers, ribbons, craft materials, poems, images and the invitation to read a short Bible passage (ancient wisdom) and create a response. An invitation to creativity.

Every Sunday, these rituals were accompanied by a quotation from the Bible, often introduced as ancient wisdom, and a quotation or statement from a famous author or proverb. We wanted to offer something ancient/future to the community. A tangible way to be present to the changing world in which we were and are continuing to live.

There is something in this experience for me which has highlighted the richness of the contemplative tradition of the church. Surrounded by family life—home-schooling toddlers is a riot between glue-sticks and CBeebies—I discovered for myself the spiritual sustenance from ancient rites, rituals and practices, which have restored my equilibrium (if not always quelled my anxiety). If these ancient gifts of our Christian tradition were becoming important for me, I wanted to offer them to the wider community.

The inspiration for offering something as a blessing and response for the community to participate in together was itself a gift of the online world. As colleagues all began to run towards the video camera, much was mourned as church buildings closed their doors. I was particularly struck by an article by Meg Warner, reflecting on ritual, response and the search for the sacred in the face of trauma and tragedy:

> In the days, weeks and months that followed the string of tragedies, large numbers of ordinary people availed themselves of memorial services, public cleansing rites, and opportunities to participate in simple public rituals. Not only the public, but local authorities and government looked to the [church] to help them in their responses to the disasters… [In London] the Borough Council approached the Dean of Southwark for advice about how to deal with an impromptu 'shrine' of flowers, Post-it notes and teddy bears that had built up, *à la* Princess Diana, on London Bridge and that was quickly becoming a public health hazard. Andrew Nunn arranged for a very brief public liturgy at the site, designed to smooth the removal of the gathered items into trucks, and to reassure the passing public that the items would be not just relegated to the status of rubbish, but treated with respect. The intention was that once he had picked up one, totemic, item and placed it on the truck, professional staff would step in to complete the transfer. That was not what happened. Instead, the gathered members of the public, entirely of their own accord, formed a queue and one by one picked up items and took them reverently to the trucks. They created their own ritual, and so a potential PR disaster was turned into an opportunity for healing and integration.[28]

COVID-19 is a trauma and a tragedy in its own right. However, if this was the case for other incidents of deep community bereavement and lament, I began to question what role could ritual play in our community for the present? Especially at a time when all the usual rituals (church worship, hymnody, and even funerals) were themselves alien or absent.

In Warner's contribution, I found challenge, solace and permission to be bold, to offer something to the community—and as a member of the clergy, dare I suggest that I found something to offer to God; perhaps even something graced and sacramental in both the offering and the receiving.

Serendipitously, our wayside pulpit to our passing community has brought Sabbath and the practices of Sabbath into the subconscious of those who take the time to pause—both online and off. John Swinton has noted that in order to move from scarcity to generosity in the midst of lockdown, one of the strongest gifts of faith communities is the practice of Sabbath.[29] Our Sabbath Sunday self-care proclamations preach hope, share Jesus and invite soulfulness with the intention of enabling the flourishing of our community. At a time when I and my colleagues have been turning to a pixelated pulpit, I wanted to find a way to embody my own vulnerability, anxiety and despair—and to follow the nudge of God to consider the community at my gatepost as the congregation since the majority of my congregation are literally locked away from view.[30]

Embracing Anonymity

This is precisely why this chapter appears in a book about meeting God online. What I have begun to (un)learn is the power of anonymity in the online world; the power which unexpectedly comes from being out of sight or away from view.

The taking of a Sabbath is as much about letting the self be the self as it is about letting God be God. Missionally, therefore, the use of a Sunday, the offer of meaning-making, and the invitation to soul care all contribute to a re-imagination of what anonymity online might enable, rather than disable.[31] Anonymity has become something of our genius. Other than putting a single photograph on my personal and church Facebook pages, I have deliberately not created a social campaign. Oftentimes, the contributions are the result of last-minute wrangling about what might get put out next. As a result of this intentional anonymity, I have watched as images of our wayside, gatepost pulpit appear on local community group forums, Snapchat and even referenced in blog posts around the world. What we have offered has gained more interest, greater reach and a generosity from the community than would have happened if I had sought shares, retweets, engagements or interest from mission partners and organisations.

Taking a Sabbath is as much about letting the self be the self as letting God be God

In a world where we count impact by clicks and likes, it is tempting to be seduced by the dopamine high of click-success. I have discovered that by remaining anonymous, and intentionally not engaging with posts about what we are doing, two things have happened. The first is that my soul care is in check. This is not a competitive ego trip; this is an invitation to engage in a practical, embodied, ritual response to offer hope in a fearful world. Secondly, it has made me braver in following the scent of the creative, wild Spirit, in mission from our driveway.

It may seem counterintuitive, but anonymity has power. Recognized and used well, I am discovering that something rooted in a physical, tactile response actually gains momentum and power when it becomes viral. There is something of God's sense of humour where, in the midst of a virus, going viral is redeemed!

People now travel down our road *because* they want to engage with what is on offer. People take their own versions of pilgrimages to visit our chalkboard and plastic altar.

Conclusion

> 'I'm new around here,' said one passer-by as I set up the chalkboard one chilly morning. 'Can I ask, are you from the church? It's just that the church is always good at offering hope.'

Without ceremony or introduction, the Spirit of God is doing her thing in the community, and remaining anonymous is good for my soul. It keeps this offering Jesus-centred. It is reliant on grace and the creative flourishes of the Spirit in the midst of the anxiety, despair, trauma and tragedy that we are all facing. In turn, it seems to be drawing people into a hope-full, soul-full relationship with themselves and with God too. Each ritual opens up sacred space within people for their spirit to be revived and restored.

We have discovered the ancient/future blessing of offering worldwide wisdom, and seeing how others offer that themselves on the world wide web in ritual and response.

Closing Reflections from Peter Phillips

5

What is God Up To?

The little church of Beacon Lough in Gateshead has seen a large growth spike during the pandemic. Before the outbreak the congregation was around 50. Nowadays their online services are viewed by about 250 people regularly on YouTube and Facebook Live and for a sizeable portion of the service—they are not just jumping in and leaving. Indeed, the raw figures show much larger growth of up to 1,000 (mini-)views per week. Those numbers have been supported by small Facebook ads sending out service times and links to those living within 1km of the church's (closed) premises. Ian Britton at Premier Digital has been doing some analysis of the data and sending me regular updates, which show that the move online has offered people close to the church an opportunity to be present at worship from the comfort and security of their own homes. But it is not necessarily anonymous viewing. Often, they comment, or like the service or contact church members they know, helping the congregation to build links to these new attendees, and discover that they often have a loose connection to the church already or know someone who attended in the past. The congregation pray for these people and also encourage them into discipleship groups such as *Alpha* online. Intriguingly, the church's giving has increased as well.

Digital church is a domestic, open, safe, interactive church

Beacon Lough is a small church and it will be interesting to see how many of the new adherents come to physical church when it is re-established, but this experience is replicated across many churches in the UK and worldwide. When the church went online, she opened up a new shop window into how church is done in the contemporary world. Hybrid church is a domestic church filled with images of people's living rooms and kitchens. It is an open church which welcomes everyone whether they are dressed in their Sunday best or their pyjamas. It is a safe church where you do not have to pretend to be OK. It is an interactive church where help is at hand through phone numbers, emails and helplines for you to talk to a real person to whom you may have been introduced in the Zoom prayer ministry room or on the YouTube service.

The bigger picture of what God is up to may not be known for a while. Who can fathom the mind of God? The mission of God may be behind the focus on social justice: for more action against the curse of racism; for more action to prevent cataclysmic climate change; for more action to help the poor have equal opportunities in a world where the 1% own so much of the world's resources. God sees us praying that his kingdom might come and all of these actions are part of the wider need for societal reform, not just church reform. Closing the church building reminds us that the mission of God burst out of the temple when the veil was torn and exploded onto the streets. The Spirit blows where she wills and will not be limited by our craving for the trappings of institutionalism.

We have seen that this *church without walls* is a church of many faces: of choirs and music groups; of impromptu readers and people leading prayers; of those from BAME communities; of those doing all-age crafts; of keyworkers and COVID-19 volunteers. This is a church where the housebound are welcome, the disabled can play a full part and those in care homes are included. Church with a human face, even when that is a blackboard and table at the end of the garden path.

When you are on display digitally people see you, they see what you are about, so we pray that we are giving a genuine answer to the hope that is within us as we engage in the true mission of God (2 Pet 3.15). It reflects the Zulu traditional greeting, 'I am here,' and its response, 'I see you.' The first opens up the opportunity for engagement—for interpersonal relationship as two people look at each other eye to eye—and the response acknowledges that the person has been seen, is present, is known. It values that other person as a real human being too.

We need to acknowledge that God has been up to a lot. He says, 'I AM here' and many people have responded, 'I see you.' In many different ways, in many different instalments. We need a *church without walls* full of a rich diversity of faces (multi-racial, multi-tonal, multi-ethnic, multi-abled, multi-gendered). These faces need to announce their presence, 'I am here,' and hear the missioning God who replies, 'I see you, I acknowledge who you are. Let's journey together.'

A *church without walls* offers a God who meets us where we are and invites us to walk with him along the way.

Contributors

The Rev'd Dr Joanne Cox-Darling is a Methodist minister in South Staffordshire. She is the Chair of The Christian Enquiries Agency, which runs www.christianity.org.uk

The Rev'd Matthew Pulis is a Maltese Catholic priest, serving at the parish of Dingli and preparing to read for a doctorate in practical digital theology.

The Rev'd Bryony Taylor worked as a social media consultant before being ordained in the Church of England in 2014. She is now Rector of Barlborough and Clowne in North East Derbyshire.

Notes

1 For a selection of resources and articles see: https://durham.ac.uk/digitaltheology/COVID19

2 http://sanctuaryfirst.org.uk

3 See https://churchofscotland.org.uk/__data/assets/pdf_file/0006/11787/CWW_REPORT_for_website_2Nov2012.pdf and Sanctuary First's conference exploring the report in the context of digital culture in 2019: https://churchofscotland.org.uk/news-and-events/news/2019/sanctuary-first-conference-re-imagines-church

4 SavantaComRes for Tearfund, 3 March 2020: https://comresglobal.com/polls/tearfund-covid-19-prayer-public-omnibus-research/; Katie Harrison, Director of SavantaComRes Faith Research Centre: 'Church Services Reaching Multitudes During Lockdown,' 9 June 2020: https://comresglobal.com/church-services-reaching-multitudes-during-lockdown/

5 Peter Phillips, *The Bible, Digital Culture and Social Media* (London: Routledge Press, 2019).

6 OfCom, '2019 Report: Online Nation': https://www.ofcom.org.uk/__data/assets/pdf_file/0025/149146/online-nation-report.pdf

7 ONS data on Statista, 'Share of households with internet access 1998–2019,' 14 February 2020 [online]: https://www.statista.com/statistics/275999/household-internet-penetration-in-great-britain/

8 ONS, 'Digital Exclusion,' 4 March 2019: https://www.ons.gov.uk/peoplepopulationandcommunity/householdcharacteristics/homeinternetandsocialmediausage/articles/exploringtheuksdigitaldivide/2019-03-04#the-scale-of-digital-exclusion-in-the-uk

9 Craig von Buseck, *Netcasters: Using the Internet to Make Fishers of Men* (London: Broadman and Holman, 2010).

10 That is, she clicks 'like' on many items shared on Facebook.

11 I write in more detail about this in an essay: B Taylor, 'The Distanced Church: Reflections on Doing Church Online' in H Campbell (ed), *Digital Religion Publications-Network for New Media, Religion and Digital Culture Studies* (Texas: College Station, 2020).

12 Kate Fox, *Watching the English* (London, Hodder and Stoughton, 2004) p 357.

13 It does, of course, also open up the problem of keyboard warriors abusing people behind a secret identity, but here I am talking about the positive side to this for mission.

14 Bryony Taylor, *Sharing Faith Using Social Media* (Grove Evangelism booklet Ev115) p 7.

15 H Thurnston and A Shipman, 'The Rosary,' in *The Catholic Encyclopaedia* (New York: Robert Appleton Company, 1912).

16 Catholic Way Publishing, *The Holy Rosary* (E-Book: Catholic Way Publishing, 2013).

17 As per last census, there are only 36 non-Maltese residents.

18 National Statistics Office, 'Census of Population and Housing 2011: Final Report' (Valletta, Malta: National Statistics Office, 2014).

19 Elise Ann Allen, 'Pope Urges Families to Pray Rosary Together during Month of May,' *Crux*, April 2020.

20 *ibid.*

21 Thomas O'Loughlin, 'We Are Celebrants, Not Consumers,' *La Croix* ('La Croix: Nottingham, May 2020).

22 Second Vatican Council, '*Lumen Gentium: Dogmatic Constitution on the Church,*' (Vatican: Vatican Press, 1964) para 68.

23 Fulton Sheen, *The World's First Love* (San Francisco, CA: Ignatius Press, 2nd ed, 2009) p 164.

24 Pope Francis. 'Prayer of the Holy Father to Mary for the Month of May.' Vatican Press, 25 April 2020: http://www.vatican.va/content/francesco/en/prayers/documents/papa-francesco_preghiere_20200425_preghiera-mariana-maggio.html

25 J Thayer and W Smith, *The NAS New Testament Greek Lexicon* (biblestudytools.com, 1999).

26 It is worth stating that each of these offerings was done with considered risks of cross contamination: 72 hours in the planning, wrapped or wiped where possible.

27 https://sojo.net/articles/shane-clabornes-12-hopes-2012

28 Meg Warner, 'Revisiting Aberfan—The Church of England and COVID-19': https://megwarner.wixsite.com/bible/post/2020/05/05/re-visiting-aberfan-the-church-of-england-and-covid-19

29 J Swinton, 'Theology in a Time of Covid': https://vimeo.com/425415436

30 This is an intentional nod towards the work of Brene Brown, who has shown empirically that vulnerability is the vehicle to wholeness and soulfulness.

31 See D Kessler, *Finding Meaning* (London: Penguin, 2019).